ABERDEENSHIRE TRAMWAYS

A delightfully lively view of Castle Street in 1891, looking up Union Street to the west. The Mercat Cross is the circular structure in the foreground, with a mattress and other second-hand goods for sale in front of it. Behind that is the cabman's shelter and behind that the Duke of Gordon's statue. On the left is the pillared portico of the Royal Athenaeum with a line of cabs waiting for trade, and on the right the North of Scotland Bank with the Tollbooth and Towns House behind. Two Aberdeen District horse trams are almost the only traffic around. (Postcard)

ABERDEENSHIRE
TRAMWAYS

MIKE MITCHELL

AMBERLEY

First published 2013

Amberley Publishing
The Hill, Stroud
Gloucestershire, GL5 4EP

www.amberley-books.com

British Library Cataloguing in Publication Data.
A catalogue record for this book is available from the British Library.

ISBN 978 1 4456 1382 6
ISBN 978 1 4456 1393 2

Typeset in 10pt on 12pt Sabon.
Typesetting and Origination by Amberley Publishing.
Printed in the UK.

The crossroads of Union Street, Market Street and St Nicholas Street in 1919. 1903 BEC cars 38 and 33 are heading for Castle Street, preceded by the almost new 84 on a shuttle to Sea Beach, Visible on the right is the 'Beach Lye', a siding used to queue Beach trams clear of the main line until the capacity of the Castle Street terminus was expanded in 1937. (Postcard)

The preserved horse car, 'No. 1' (although actually 61 or 63), headed the procession to commemorate the Jubilee of tramways on 1 September 1924. This scene at Queens Cross depot could have been mistaken for the final District Tramways procession in 1898 but for the uniform of the motorman standing in front of the tram, and the edge of an electric car just visible on the left. Lord Provost William Meff is driving. (First Aberdeen)

Aberdeen and the First Railways

One of the four largest Scottish towns, the city of Aberdeen lies between the Rivers Dee and Don, on the north-east coast some 130 miles north of Edinburgh and 70 miles from the nearest comparably sized community, Dundee. It is an ancient settlement, having been noted as 'Devana' on Ptolemy's map of North Britain in AD 146. By the end of the sixteenth century, the city had a population of over 4,000 and was a recognised seat of learning, the first of its two rival universities having been founded in 1495. Seaborne trade had been an important part of the local economy since early days. In 1656 there were nine Aberdeen-based vessels, ranging from 20 tons to 80 tons capacity, but by 1692 the Aberdeen fleet consisted of only two ships of 30 tons capacity each. The principal manufactured exports from Aberdeen in the seventeenth century were of tweed cloth, other exports being mainly of surplus agricultural produce and livestock.

The completion of the railway line to Aberdeen in 1850 led to a further opening up of Aberdeenshire to the wider market, and in particular easy access to the west coast and inland areas of Britain. For the first time also, perishable meat and fish could be sent dependably to the London markets within thirty-six hours. Construction of railways within the north-east of Scotland increased the penetration of the Aberdeenshire economy by the wider market, as well as increasing the size of the local market. Prior to the construction of the Great North of Scotland Railway between Aberdeen and Elgin, together with the rural branches often constructed by minor companies which were then absorbed by the Great North, the transport network in north-east Scotland consisted of a short length of canal between Aberdeen and Inverurie and considerable lengths of turnpike road, constructed since the 1790s. Although these roads were a major advance on what had gone before, the difficulties affecting goods transport in particular restricted the ability or the inclination of rural producers to engage in the wider market. The railways changed the situation quite dramatically, and the 291 miles in operation by 1870, with stations in virtually every village of any size (as well as some in open countryside), meant that few producers were more than a mile or two from a railhead.

The effect of these developments on the population of Aberdeenshire was profound. As agricultural production changed from labour-intensive arable farming to livestock production, and as the scale of industrial processes in Aberdeen in

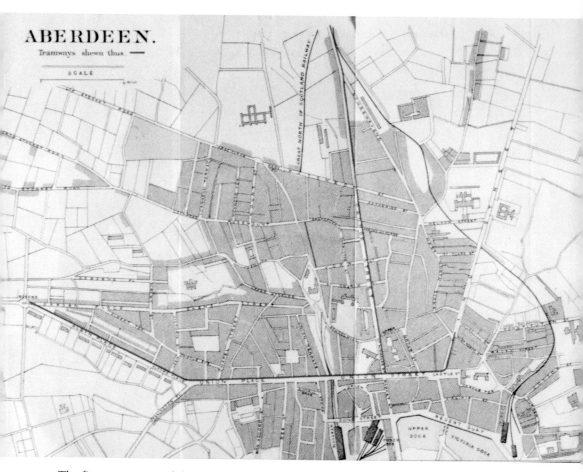

The first two routes of the Aberdeen District Tramways were from North Church to Queens Cross and Kittybrewster. The map also illustrates the limited extent of urban development in the mid-1870s. (First Aberdeen)

particular increased, the incentive for the rural population to migrate to Aberdeen or even further afield increased. The increase in the population of Aberdeen as industrial and processing industries grew was spectacular. In common with most other British cities, Aberdeen experienced a dramatic increase in population in the 150 years after 1801. The census of 1801 indicated a population of 26,992; this had doubled by 1831, and had almost doubled again by 1881.

The growth in population was accompanied by the outward spread of the city beyond the built-up area which had constituted the city since medieval days.

The Horse Buses

The first attempt to operate a regular bus service on a fixed timetabled route at fixed fares seems to have been a short-lived experiment with a steam bus which operated from Broadford (now Hutcheon Street) up the hill to Kittybrewster Toll from September 1833. The idea was to prove the reliability of the bus before putting it into service on a route from Aberdeen to Ballater, but the service came to an abrupt end when the boiler exploded. A more conventional approach was taken by J. Donaldson, who started what he described as the first regular bus service in Aberdeen on an infrequent network of routes to Old Aberdeen, Woodside, Footdee, and the Leith steamer terminal at the docks on 1 May 1839. It is clear from press reports that buses were operating to Woodside, Old Aberdeen and the canal terminus at Kittybrewster in the 1840s and 1850s. By 1866 one of the hackney cab operators, William Bain, had introduced bus services to Bieldside, Blairs and between Queens Cross and Old Aberdeen, though even the most frequent (to Bieldside) only ran every two hours. Although the development of the Aberdeen District horse trams from 1874 gradually supplanted not only Bain's buses but those of the several other operators who had appeared by the 1880s, the horse bus network was a significant part of public transport provision in Aberdeen until the early 1890s. The last one – to Blairs – was withdrawn in 1920.

The Horse Trams

The original horse tramway lines of the Aberdeen District Tramways Company, opened in 1874 between Queens Cross and North Church, and St Nicholas Street and Causewayend, covered the city as it then existed, and only the Queens Cross area was in any sense an underdeveloped area. In 1875 the City of Aberdeen Land Association was founded and started development of the Fountainhall area, and similar residential development in the Mannofield area led to the extension of the tramways there in 1880, along with extensions to the King Street line, and a connection to Woodside, until 1891 a separate burgh. Development in the south of the city led to a further extension to Bloomfield in 1883, while the construction of the Rosemount viaduct over the Denburn Valley in 1883 made the construction of a horse tramway through Rosemount a practical proposition. In 1894 route extensions were completed to the Bridge of Dee and the Bridge of Don, and two years later a short extension was built to reach the Bayview area of Queens Road.

By 1890 it was clear that the further expansion of Aberdeen as an urban centre was dependent on a faster and cheaper replacement for the horse tramways.

Within the city, population movements were taking place as the more prosperous citizens purchased houses in the developing west end of Aberdeen, leaving the congested city-centre wards to those unable to move. The role of the Aberdeen District Tramways in promoting this movement of population within the city was crucial, but not unique, as the number of horse bus services in operation in the city testified. The fares were, however, higher than could be afforded by most of the citizens, and it is clear from contemporary comment that the only members of the labouring classes likely to ride on some routes were the crew.

A very early view of Woodside No. 4 at St Nicholas Street with a young Queen Victoria surveying the scene. The horses have been taken for watering. (Postcard)

Construction of the more easily graded Rosemount Viaduct in 1883 had allowed the District to extend the horse tram network from Queens Cross via Mile End to Union Terrace. This car is turning onto Union Street at Castle Street. North Church, the original terminus of the Queens Cross line, can be seen directly behind the tram. (Postcard)

An early view of a Queens Cross horse car passing the queen's statue at St Nicholas Street on its way along Union Street. The imposing Town House tower (completed in 1874) is behind. (Postcard)

The Bayview extension from Queens Cross took the horse trams another half-mile along Queens Road, past the new villas visible behind. Had the Skene and Echt tramway been built, it would have branched off to the right near here, across what were still open fields at this time. This car is at Bayview terminus, and incidentally shows the state of the road beyond the tramway-maintained cobbled surface. (First Aberdeen)

Kittybrewster No. 5 at St Nicholas Street terminus. The section of line between here and
Schoolhill was always single with passing loops, and contributed to the decision to close the
route in 1955. Note, the statue of Queen Victoria has been remodelled to show an older queen.
(Postcard)

Aberdeen Corporation Tramways

Municipal ownership of the tramways had been considered as a possibility from the earliest days of the Aberdeen District Tramways Company, but the first time the subject was seriously suggested was in the Town Council elections of 1892. A statement by the company that they would not promote 'any great extension', and also by implication that no conversion to mechanical propulsion would be undertaken, led Lord Provost Mearns to table a proposal for purchase in November 1895, and call for a 'response' from the Tramway Company.

The initial Corporation offer of £15 per share was considered inadequate by the company, and negotiations were broken off after the Corporation finance committee recommended the offer be reduced to £14 per share. Despite the company's stated reluctance to extend its network, a short route extension to Bayview from Queens Cross was undertaken in 1896, and this may have encouraged the Great North of Scotland Railway to make a final offer to purchase the tramways, as 'they might be worked in conjunction with its proposed railway to Skene and Echt [see below], and other light railways into the country'. The Bayview line would have formed a part of the Skene line. How serious the GNSR were is somewhat doubtful, since there is evidence that the railway company was attempting to forestall the proposals for several light railway schemes for the area which were then in circulation by promoting its own, often financially impracticable, schemes. Certainly, by proposing that its own Skene line would operate down Queens Road, in the prosperous west end of the city, the GNSR seemed to be inviting the implacable opposition of the Town Council. Although a price of £16 per share was quickly agreed with the District Tramways, there was no prospect of gaining Town Council agreement, and the Council even refused to meet the railway company to discuss the matter. The terms of the formal refusal of consent to the purchase give an interesting insight into the Town Council's motivation. Three reasons were given: the Town Council wanted to run its own system as representatives of the ratepayers, the success of the Glasgow municipalisation was clear evidence of the success of local authority operation of tramways, and the financial and other benefits which should flow to the ratepayers, not shareholders.

The District Tramways passed into the ownership of Aberdeen Corporation on 26 August 1898, and this was welcomed by the local press without exception.

Aberdeenshire Tramway Schemes

During the latter half of the nineteenth century there were a number of schemes for rural tramways in Aberdeenshire, as well as a number of light railway schemes designed to increase conventional railway penetration of the countryside. None of these schemes came to fruition, but two of the most interesting (and tramway-like) were the projected steam line to Newburgh and Peterhead, and the competing steam and electric proposals for a tramway to Echt.

The Aberdeen–Newburgh–Peterhead Steam Tramway was proposed in June 1876 by a group of Aberdeenshire merchants, largely as a means of transporting Peterhead granite to the Aberdeen finishing works. The route would have been from the Caledonian Railway station in Guild Street via the Quays, Bridge of Don and through Belhelvie, Newburgh, Collieston, Slains and Cruden to Boddam and Peterhead, with a possible alternative route via Colthill Loch and along the road-side to the Peterhead turnpike road. Motive power was to be steam, using a self-contained Porteous & Bruce patent steam car, a double-deck open-top six-wheeler which weighed 2 tons, and which was claimed to be able to climb a 1-in-16 gradient and stop within its own length. This single-ended vehicle was turned by lowering an extra wheel kept under the back platform, raising the rear wheels off the ground, and pushing the car round, using the four-wheel bogie as a pivot. A further scheme in September 1877 also failed, as did a GNSR proposal for a line to Newburgh, connecting with the city tramways.

Various schemes for a tramway to Echt and Midmar were floated between 1877 and the early years of the twentieth century. The Aberdeen, Skene, Echt and Midmar Tramways were floated in late 1877 with a standard gauge steam line from Midmar via Echt and Rubsilaw to Woolmanhill and Schoolhill. Although local authorities were generally sympathetic, the promoters were unable to satisfy Aberdeen Corporation's reservations about the route being too narrow and steep for steam locomotives. A new scheme, the Aberdeenshire Light Railways, was proposed in 1896. This standard gauge steam line would have run from Echt on private right of way to the city boundary at Woodend, with a branch to Skene village. Inside the city, the route would have run down to the District tramway terminus at Bayview, before branching across fields to the end of Union Grove and then via various back streets to join the Harbour Board lines in Market Street. The scheme was withdrawn in favour of the Echt Light Railway, another similar scheme promoted by the Great North of Scotland Railway, also in 1896, from Echt to the Bayview tram terminus. Both these latter schemes were strongly opposed by Aberdeen Corporation. The GNSR attempted to overcome this by promoting lines from Woodend to Kittybrewster (abandoned because of very high costs) and to Mannofield and Holburn Street station. The scheme was dropped in December 1898 after the Aberdeen District Tramways were purchased by the Corporation. Finally, in 1900 the Skene & Echt Light Railway was proposed by the Aberdeen District Committee of Aberdeen County Council. Their proposal for a roadside line from Woodend to Echt was similar to the GNSR scheme, but with a branch to Waterton (Dunecht). Estimates for electric and steam standard and 3 ft 6 in. gauge schemes were obtained, but the costs were prohibitive. GNSR motor buses arrived in the area in June 1905 (from Culter) and a direct service to Schoolhill station, Aberdeen, started in September 1906.

Two tramways which were built were the Strabathie Light Railway and the Cruden Bay Hotel Tramway.

The Strabathie Light Railway was an industrial tramway built in 1899 to connect the Seaton Brick & Tile Company brickworks at Black Dog, which had been constructed the previous year, with the Bridge of Don. Although the line was 3 ft gauge, the company proposed to use dual-gauge wagons to run on to the Aberdeen tramways, and for a time used ex-Aberdeen horse trams as passenger cars for its workers. Although the proposed connection with the tramways was included in the 1899 Bill, the section was withdrawn and the link was never built. When the Murcar golf course was opened in 1909, a petrol railcar was operated over the line between the golf clubhouse and the Bridge of Don by the club, and when the Seaton Brick & Tile Company went into liquidation in 1924 the line was purchased by the golf club. It continued to operate until 1950.

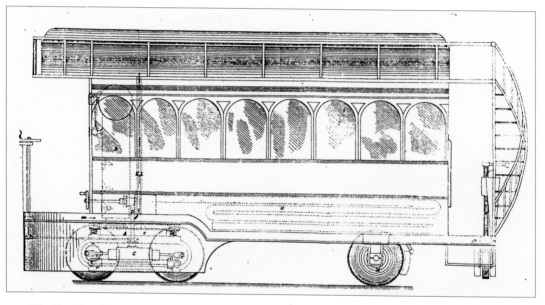

The Peterhead steam tramway was to be operated by this six-wheeled Porteous steam car.

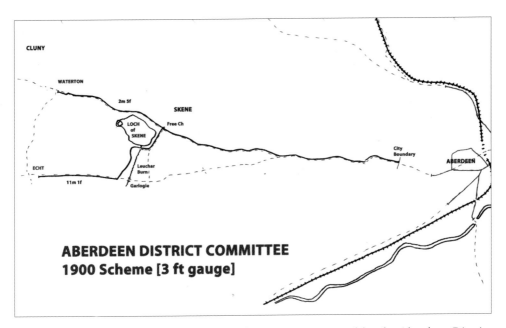

The last of the Skene and Echt tramway schemes was promoted by the Aberdeen District Committee of the County Council. Waterton is now named Dunecht.

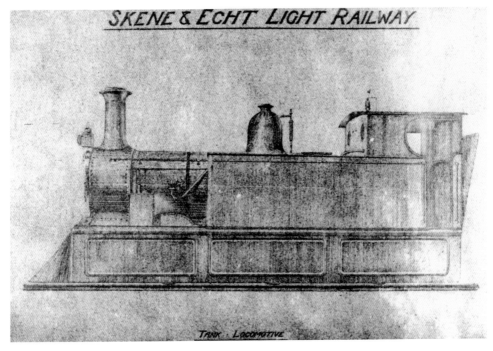

Maker's drawing of the tank engines planned for the Skene & Echt Light Railway. The prospect of these locomotives steaming past the newly developing and highly fashionable villas of Queens Road with trains of goods wagons drew implacable opposition to both the Aberdeenshire Light Railways and the Great North of Scotland Railway schemes from Aberdeen Corporation.

A proposed Skene & Echt coach.

The Murcar 'buggie' ran three or four trips a day between the Bridge of Don and the Murcar Golf Club, some 2 miles north. This vehicle was built by J. B. Duff of Aberdeen in 1909. The box on the roof is the radiator.

A posed photo of one of the two Cruden Bay trams near the front door of the hotel. Livery was red, white and green. The comparison between the smart hotel staff and the driver is noticeable. The round top of the unusual Maley & Taunton power controller, operated by a vertically mounted handle, can be seen behind the dash panel.

Cruden Bay Hotel Tramway

In January 1895, the GNSR Board decided to look into the possibility of building a luxury hotel near Port Erroll on the Buchan coast north of Ellon. By the end of that month, estimates and plans were submitted for the 'Port Erroll Hotel', as the Cruden Bay Hotel was known as first. It was to be a fifty-five-bedroom structure, built of pink Peterhead granite at a cost of £13,816. Perhaps conscious of the distance of their new hotel from the station (over half a mile) and the need to offer the latest in comforts to the top-class guest whose custom they were aiming for, the GNSR Finance Committee decided, in August 1898, to send the directors and the company's engineers to the Isle of Man to inspect the 'Electric and Light Railways' there. The delegation must have been impressed, for on 14 September 1898, the Board 'considered further plans for a laundry, a combined passenger and luggage lift and an electrical tramway between the hotel and the station including an extra engine and dynamo at Cruden Bay'. The cost was put at £9,005. The hotel opened for guests at the beginning of March 1899 amid much press attention, and the tramway three months later.

The tramway was constructed very much as a railway with trams running on it. The track was bullhead rail on chaired sleepers, with open ballasted formation between the road crossing and the station yard. At the hotel and in the station yard, the track was paved to rail level with granite setts. The gauge was a nominal 3 ft 6 ins.

Although profitable in its early years, the Cruden Bay Hotel soon became an embarrassment to its owners, and never achieved the profit levels of the other two GNSR hotels, the 'Palace' and the 'Station' in Aberdeen. The remoteness of the place, and its dependence on the weather and on a specialised well-to-do clientèle, made its chances of success poor from the start. When the Boddam line was closed to passengers in 1932, the main reason for the tramway's existence was taken away, and the hotel's isolation was made complete in the days before mass motoring. The LNER provided a limousine service to Aberdeen in 1934, using a Rolls-Royce, and the trams continued to carry laundry baskets and coal until the army requisitioned the hotel in March 1941. Thereupon the tramway was dismantled for scrap, and the hotel itself, failing to find a buyer after the army vacated it in 1945, was demolished between 1947 and 1952. One of the trams still exists and is on display, fully restored, at the Grampian Transport Museum at Alford.

Building the Electric Tramway System: 1898–1905

During the months immediately following the purchase of the District Tramways by Aberdeen Corporation, the tramway undertaking continued much as before, with the routine letting of contracts and the detail of operations being managed by David Moonie, the ex-District Tramways superintendent. The future development of the tramways for the benefit of the public was the preoccupation of Councillor

Alexander Wilkie of Woodside, and within a few weeks of his appointment as Tramways Convener, a visit by the Tramways Committee to see the recently opened Springburn electric tramway in Glasgow was suggested.

By November 1899, the Woodside line was almost complete apart from a short stretch of the city-bound line near Kittybrewster, while two cars were in use on driver training. The line opened to electric traction on 23 December 1899.

Alexander Wilkie believed that while it was up to the Town Council to bring the benefits of electric tramways to its own citizens, it was not their duty to risk the city's money on lines outside the boundary. In his speech at the opening of the Woodside line, he said that the Corporation's role should be to enter into operating agreements with any country lines rather than to operate them themselves, a view which fitted in very well with his other role as promoter of the Aberdeen Suburban Tramways (see below).

An expansion plan was considered by the Tramways Committee in early November 1899. In addition to conversion of the ex-District lines to Bridge of Dee, Bridge of Don, Mannofield, Rosemount and Woodside, new double-track electric lines were to be built to Ferryhill via Crown Street, Ferryhill Road, Bon-Accord Street, Fonthill Road, with a single-track branch to the Duthie Park, Torry via Bridge Street, Guild Street, South Market Street and Victoria Road, and Sea Beach via Constitution Street.

The Aberdeen Corporation Bill which was lodged in the 1899 session covered all of these conversions and extensions, as well as a short connection over the Bridge of Don to connect with the Strabathie Light Railway from Bridge of Don to Murcar, an industrial line serving a brick and tile works, but the narrow width of the bridge proved an insuperable obstacle and this proposal was withdrawn from the Bill to avoid delaying its progress. In any case, some doubts on the value of the link were beginning to emerge.

The Torry line appeared to have the greatest traffic potential from the rapid building developments in Victoria Road, where many new houses were being built for successful trawlermen and fish merchants at this time. However, the route selected lay across the harbour quays, and although the Aberdeen Harbour Commissioners had been willing to consider a double-track tramway on the section between the end of Guild Street and Victoria Bridge, the coal merchants and other traders who would have been affected succeeded in getting the line reduced to single track in the parliamentary committee's consideration of the Bill because of the likely conflict with the many carts which loaded and unloaded there, and the numerous railway crossings between the dockside lines and the railway goods yard.

Although the Sea Beach section was to be built as an overhead electrification, the electrical engineer was instructed to get cost estimates from Westinghouse for an 'underground conduit' system for Union Street, reflecting concerns expressed at the time over the visual impact of overhead wires.

The contract for the Beach line was let in October 1900, and the following month preparatory work on doubling the track in Great Western Road and on the

Rosemount Circle was authorised. However, in December 1900 an agreement was made with McElroy-Grunow Electric Railway System of Bridgeport, Connecticut, USA to install their patented surface-contact electrical collection system on the last 400 yards of the Beach route, as an experiment to prove the feasibility of the system for Union Street, and the Beach contract was modified accordingly. After numerous false starts, the McElroy-Grunow system was removed and replaced by conventional overhead wires.

The Ferryhill tramway opened at 4 p.m. on 24 June 1902, with public services starting on 26 June. The Guild Street bridge, which was being reconstructed by the Great North of Scotland Railway as part of the extension work on Aberdeen Joint passenger station, held up the completion of the Torry line and its linking to the rest of the system. The Torry line opened between Guild Street and St Fittick's Road on 10 October 1903. The inspection and opening of the Torry and Fonthill Road lines followed on 28 November 1903. The final link to Torry over the Guild Street bridge was opened on 15 July 1905.

The Aberdeen tramway system, by these developments, had virtually assumed its final form, though extensions from Bayview to Hazlehead and Woodside to Scatterburn (a re-extension over part of the Donside Suburban route) still lay in the future. The whole of the built-up extent of the city as it existed prior to the First World War was now within easy walking distance of a tramway.

Construction of the trackwork at Woodside depot in mid-1899, with two of the newly delivered trams visible. The imposing gentleman in the light coat is David Moonie, who had been manager of the District Tramways and became Tramways Superintendent with the Corporation. A more imposing granite façade was soon added to the corrugated iron shed. (*Tramway & Railway World*)

Woodside 5 was used to open the first electrified route to Woodside, and here Lord Provost Stewart is seen driving it, with Alexander Wilkie behind him. Moonie, the first Tramways Superintendent, is sitting in the corner seat directly above. The others are councillors, contractors and city officials. (First Aberdeen)

An official, posed view of Woodside 2 with motorman C. Wight at Anderson Road, a year after opening of the Woodside electric route. Initially, each route had a separate numbering series for its trams, so that there would also be a Mannofield 2, Bridges 2 and so on. Hackney Licence no. 45 is visible above the door. 2 was one of eight Brush fifty-two-seaters supplied for the first Aberdeen electric route in 1899. The last survivor was 4, which lasted as salt car 4a to 1949. (First Aberdeen)

An early form of lifeguard is fitted to Woodside 8, one of the attempts to reduce accidents due to pedestrians walking in front of cars. Morrison's Economic Stores was known to generations of Aberdonians as Raggie Morrisons, because of the cheap garments sold there. Marks & Spencer now occupy the site. (Postcard)

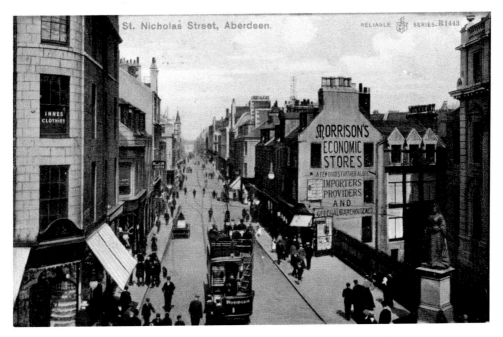

Woodside 1 waits to depart from St Nicholas Street around 1900. (Postcard)

Woodside 7 was one of the first batch of electric trams delivered in 1899 and is seen here near Woodside terminus.

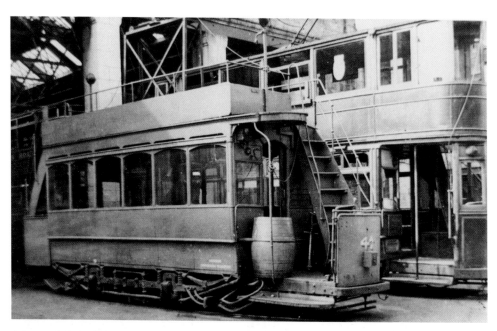

After withdrawal from passenger service in 1929, former Woodside 4 was converted to a works car and renumbered 4a. It is seen at King Street depot alongside one of the ex-Nottingham trams acquired in 1936. (Hector Mackenzie)

34 was one of the ex-District horse cars converted to electric traction and is seen here on Union Street heading for Queens Cross. Aberdeen Corporation cars were green and white, not as tinted here by the postcard manufacturer. 34 was renumbered 58 in 1903 when the large batch of thirty-two BEC cars was delivered. (Postcard)

When the Torry route opened in 1903, it was detached from the rest of the network because of railway bridge works in Guild Street, part of the remodelling work on Aberdeen Joint railway station. As a result, this flowery tram on the opening day shows 'Guild Street' and 'Victoria Road'. This is at St Fittick's Road terminus with the Council party. (First Aberdeen)

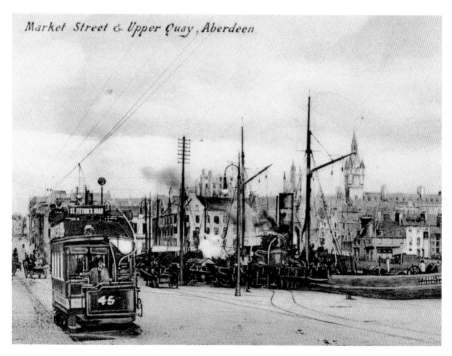

Market Street & Upper Quay, Aberdeen

The Torry route from the end of Guild Street to North Esplanade (Torry depot) was single track because of the opposition of the Aberdeen Harbour Board, which felt that a double-track line would interfere with dock operations. Here 45, a 1903 BEC car, passes a collier unloading. (Postcard)

Guild Street   Aberdeen

Because the Guild Street bridge works did not allow the Torry trams to connect with the rest of the network, out-of-service trams were stored under tarpaulins in Guild Street for a few months from October 1903 until the depot at North Esplanade was completed. The ornate building on the left is the Tivoli Theatre. (Postcard)

An excursion consisting of car 3 and four ex-horse cars (including 64, 58 and 63) crossing Victoria Bridge. Either 63 or its sister 61 was eventually renumbered 1, and led the closure ceremony in 1958. No. 1 can be seen in the Grampian Transport Museum at Alford. (First Aberdeen)

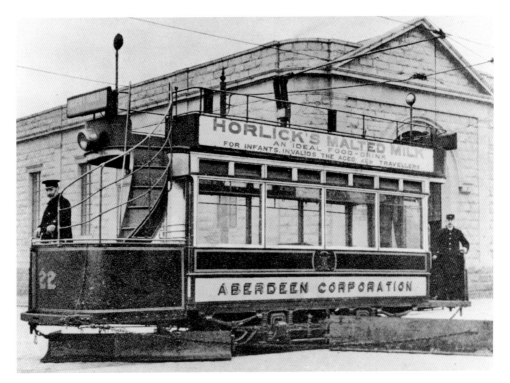

Cars 21–24 were part of an order for twelve cars from BEC which were not delivered in accordance with Aberdeen's specification and were always known as the 'Narrow Cars' because, among other defects, they were 5 inches narrower than specified. Eventually, Aberdeen agreed to take four of the completed cars, while two others were resold to the Liverpool & Prescot Light Railway, where they became 42 and 43. 22 is shown in front of Torry depot (along with Beach depot, one of the two Aberdeen tram depots still surviving), demonstrating a new design of snowplough. (First Aberdeen)

10 leads two other cars in Castle Street on an excursion to Bridge of Don. 9–20 were Brush cars with Brill 21E trucks. An abortive attempt was made to preserve car 14 in the 1960s, and more recently another of the batch is being rescued from ninety years as a house. (First Aberdeen)

An unidentifiable ex-horse car at the Bathing Station. Note the large crowds. (Postcard)

The only known photograph taken inside Dee Village (Ferryhill) depot. 26 has hit something, and ex-horse 57 is visible on the left. Ex-horse car 62, which was initially reserved for Council inspections and having been painted white was called the 'White' or 'Council' car, was stored here for many years, only being used to transport Dee Village staff to the top of Crown Street at shift changes, and consequently evaded the camera.

Another ex-horse car – 59 – at the Bathing Station (Corporation Baths) soon after the opening of the route. (First Aberdeen)

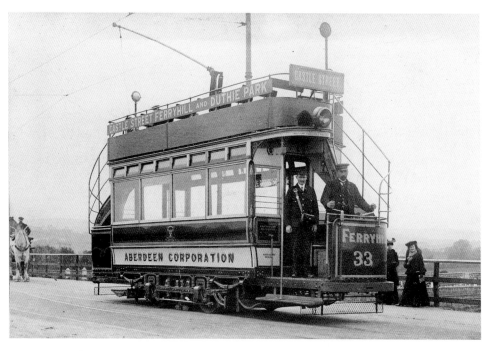

An ACT posed view of 33, a new 1903 BEC car fitted with a screw-slipper brake for use on the steeply graded Ferryhill route. At this time the fleet name was 'Aberdeen Corporation', later changed to 'Corporation Tramways'. The location is Whinhill Road, the branch for the Duthie Park. (First Aberdeen)

Overenthusiastic tinting has hidden the identities of the two Corporation cars and one Suburban car behind 18, a 1900–1 Brush fifty-two-seater. (Postcard)

Queens Cross 11 at Bridge Street around 1902. (Postcard)

Views of the Union Terrace Gardens from the Trades Hall were favourites of postcard manufacturers over the years. At the far end of the Gardens are St Mark's Church (1892, with the dome), the Central Library (1891, to its left) and Her Majesty's Theatre (1904–8, to its right). The open-top tram is an ex-horse car converted to electric between 1900 and 1902. (Postcard)

54 on Union Bridge, heading for Castle Street from Rosemount. The Great North of Scotland Railway Palace Hotel behind was destroyed by fire during the Second World War, though not as a result of enemy action.

The Aberdeen Suburban Tramways Company

The only significant population centres beyond the reach of the Aberdeen Corporation trams were the industrial villages of lower Donside between Dyce and Scatterburn, and on Deeside the suburbs of Cults and Bieldside, and the paper mill town of Culter. The first press reports of an electric tramway scheme to the suburbs appeared in the autumn of 1901, and Wilkie was deeply involved.

One of the first priorities for the new Company after the passage of its Act in 1902 was to establish through-running and power supply agreements with the Corporation, since the success of the tramway would depend largely on access to the city centre via the Mannofield and Woodside Corporation routes, and on the financial terms which could be agreed. The through-running issue was settled fairly quickly. After some talk of a joint service on Donside, with Corporation cars running to Bankhead, agreement was reached on the basis of through running by Suburban cars only.

Although the Company might have wished otherwise, the AST was destined by force of circumstances to be dependent on the Corporation Electricity Department for power supply. The Corporation were already well-established in electricity supply on Donside. On Deeside the Cults Electrical Supply Company was struggling, and the AST did not have the finance to provide its own supply, even if the obvious difficulty of supplying two physically separate routes could have been overcome.

Although the Donside line was to be built, difficulties in raising finance meant that the Deeside line would have to be severely curtailed, even though the directors were anxious to get to Bieldside at least.

The Suburban Company eventually opened its Deeside line between Mannofield Corporation tram terminus and Bieldside on 23 June 1904 and the Donside line, from Woodside tram terminus to Bankhead, on 8 July 1904.

A nearly new Suburban car 8 of 1905 is followed by ACT 18 and 43 at the east end of Union Street around 1906. (Postcard)

Alexander Wilkie (1854–1927), Aberdeen Corporation Tramways Convener 1898–1902, and then City Treasurer; managing director, Aberdeen Suburban Tramways 1904–14 and then manager until 1927. (*Bon-Accord and Northern Pictorial*)

Two of the original Suburban trams were open-topped (1 and 5) and remained so throughout their lives. The driver, George Cruickshank, and his conductor have been joined by Inspector Kerr on car 5 at the entrance to the Corporation depot at Mannofield about 1905. The ACT water sprinkler car can be glimpsed behind.

Shortly after the opening of the Suburban tramway to Donside (Bankhead), car 1 heads out of town at Bucksburn corner. (Postcard)

Car 5 near Quaker's Bridge in Bucksburn shortly after the tramway opened. Livery was red and white, matching the tinting of this card. (Postcard)

Aberdeen Suburban 5 negotiates the bend at Cults Post Office in about 1906. The pole in front of the blacksmiths shop was to become the subject of legal action between the owner of the motor garage it later became and the Suburban because the garage owner claimed it had been put there without permission. It is also the pole which allegedly electrocuted a dog which found it irresistible! (Postcard)

The 'pretty curtains' in this new Aberdeen Suburban car's non-smoking compartment are very much in evidence, as is the informal dress of the conductor. Suburban crews were not issued with uniforms until the Corporation complained about their appearance.

A very unusual shot of a tram under maintenance: Suburban 6 in Mannofield depot (where the workshops were located) with the horse-drawn overhead maintenance tower behind. It looks as if the depot has suffered a minor flood.

Car 11 heading west through Cults village. (Postcard)

Corporation Tramways Consolidation: 1905–14

By the end of the electrification phase of the Corporation Tramways development, with lines built to Torry and Ferryhill, transport provision within Aberdeen had caught up with the city's building development. However, the introduction of electric traction with higher capacity, greater speed and lower fares enabled residential development to be considered at much greater distances from the city centre than previously, and that would be a factor of great significance in developing housing strategies for post-First World War Aberdeen.

In the years to the outbreak of war in 1914, the priorities of the tramways department were to improve the service and modernise the tramcars by fitting top covers and windscreens, and by lengthening the wheelbase of the trucks to reduce the 'rocking' or 'galloping' motion from which many of the early cars suffered. The opening of the new repair shops at Dee Village Road in 1904, replacing the inadequate workshop at Woodside, meant that such tasks were well within the capabilities of the department.

By 1911 the city was once again expanding beyond the existing tramway network and proposals were being floated to cater for this. The first such plan was in April 1911, when it was remitted to the Tramways Committee to investigate a line to Footdee. This shipbuilding and fishing village at the mouth of the Dee was hardly a new development, but it had long been a conspicuous gap in the transport network, and a demand existed for improving the transport of workers from Torry and elsewhere. The tramways general manager, R. Stuart Pilcher, finally reported on the proposal in June the following year, recommending strongly against construction as being unlikely to be profitable. The Tramways Committee was unwilling to drop the scheme, however, and Pilcher was instructed to examine a trolleybus option.

Further recognition of the expansion of the city beyond the existing network was the decision to seek powers for tramway extensions to Midstocket, Menzies Road and Union Grove, as well as powers to develop motor bus routes and two trolleybus lines to Footdee and Forresterhill.

One of the most innovative developments introduced by Pilcher at this time was the Pay As You Enter (PAYE) method of fare collection, which was inaugurated on the Woodside route on 28 April 1913 with six new specially adapted trams and four rebuilt 1912 cars. The system originated on the Montreal Street Railway, where Pilcher had for a time been employed, and had been developed there by two expatriate Scots named Ross and MacDonald. The International P-A-Y-E Tramcar Company Ltd, based in London, had been formed to exploit the British and European rights to the system, and had already persuaded Leicester Corporation Tramways to install the method on its trams. In a report to the Tramways Committee, printed in full in *Tramway and Railway World*, Pilcher described the advantages of the system, which involved the conductor being stationed on the rear platform at all times and charging passengers their fares as they boarded. The major advantages claimed for the system were that every fare would be collected, platform accidents would be reduced and that journey times would be reduced, leading to fewer trams being needed to maintain the service.

The revenue on the Woodside route increased by around 2 per cent, but reaction from the public and the staff appears to have been mixed, and P-A-Y-E was abandoned in 1915.

The experimental top cover fitted to 16 earned it the nickname *Jumbo*, and it remained unique. Here it passes one of the Aberdeen Suburban open-toppers at the Palace Hotel on Union Street. Only the AST cars were really red and white in this tinted postcard. (Postcard)

Another favourite postcard location was St Nicholas Street, terminus of Woodside route 7. 1902 BEC car 30 has by now acquired a top cover, dating the photo to sometime between 1905 and the First World War. (Postcard)

Brush car 15 at Mannofield Church with its new top cover, around 1908. The points lead to Mannofield depot.

The Torry route crossed the Dee by the Victoria Bridge, which had been built in 1881 to replace a ferry. Here a 1902–3 BEC car with a Shinnie top cover makes its way into Aberdeen around 1905. (Postcard)

16 and two BEC cars at Mannofield terminus. (Postcard)

16 followed by Brush car 11 approaching Belmont Street on Union Street. (Postcard)

Brush car 9 approaches Castle Street on a Rosemount working, while 20 leaves for Mannofield around 1910. (Postcard)

1899 Brush car 8 had changed its appearance considerably by the time this shot was taken on George Street in around 1911. (Postcard)

BEC car 40 passing the Music Hall on Union Street on an inbound Mannofield working. (Postcard)

In March 1912 47 was fitted with a windscreen to a design patented by R. Stuart Pilcher, the general manager. It is seen in Whinhill Road displaying the opening flap for the driver to see forward in the rain, and the folding lower half intended to clear the handbrake handle. (First Aberdeen)

Queens Cross is the location for this tartan card of car 29 on its way to Bayview. 29 was one of the two cars fitted with experimental top covers in August 1904 (the other being 16). The rest of the fleet was fitted with covers similar to this one, but with extended canopies. 29 received an extended canopy within a few years and lasted to about 1946. (Postcard)

The Valentine's tinting has eliminated all but one contact wire in this view at Mile End on the Rosemount Circle. (First Aberdeen)

72 is seen posed with 'passengers' (probably employees from Queens Cross depot) in this demonstration of the 'Pay As You Enter' system in 1913. The PAYE system remained controversial in Aberdeen and did not long survive the First World War. 72 was rebuilt with normal stairs in 1920/21 and was scrapped in 1952. (First Aberdeen)

72 was later given a vestibule and more powerful motors to combat pirate bus competition. By the time of this view, it had also received a Peckham P35 truck. The driver is using his point iron to change the points for Mannofield at the junction of Holburn Street and Great Western Road. (RJS Wiseman)

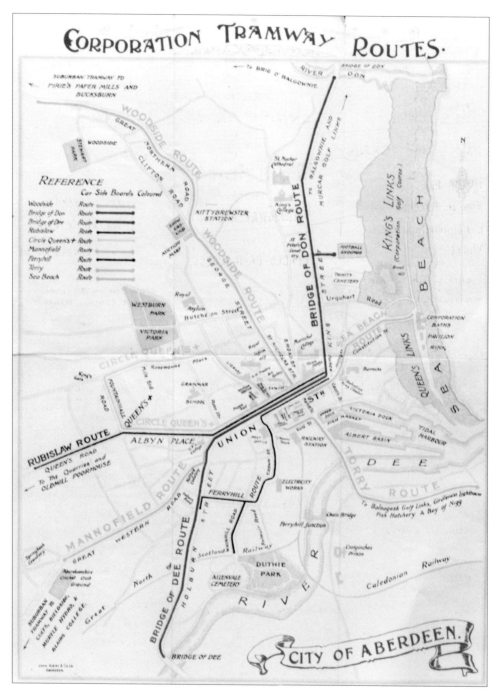

This colourful map was published by the Tramways Department and shows the route colours, which by then were displayed as lights and coloured bands on the trams at top-deck level. (First Aberdeen)

The First Purchase Attempt of the Suburban Tramways by Aberdeen Corporation

The years to the start of the First World War, and even until mid-1917, were reasonably prosperous ones for the Suburban, with a steady flow of cash into the reserve (which stood at £14,000 in mid-1914) and repayment of all the mortgages of £8,000 by 1912. Traffic levels were high and increasing, and the *Aberdeen Journal* noted in August 1913 that between 66,000 and 70,000 used the service in some weeks. According to the returns made to the Board of Trade, the only years when less than 2 million passengers were carried were 1904, when the lines opened, and 1906, when an atrocious summer had forced the numbers of passengers below the 1 million mark.

To several members of Aberdeen Town Council, the obvious answer to their problems with the Suburban was to absorb the Company lines into the Tramways Department. The leading exponent of this idea was the Tramways Convener, Councillor Smith, who floated the idea in March 1914 and formally raised it at a Council meeting on 5 October 1914. As a result, Pilcher was told to prepare a report on the subject.

Pilcher enthusiastically recommended purchase on the basis of a book valuation of £30,412.

The attitude of the Suburban was mixed; if the price was right they would sell, but they were by no means anxious to part with their tramway, which they valued at £42,000. To value the Company independently, the Tramways Department retained James Dalrymple, general manager of Glasgow Corporation Tramways, and he presented his report in late 1915 after paying two visits to the Suburban. The Tramways Committee reported his findings to the full Council on 31 January 1916, but the Dalrymple valuation of £38,000 was considerably more than the Corporation were prepared to pay, and 'the inopportune circumstances prevailing at present' (the war) were used as an excuse for shelving the whole thing.

The Suburban was not unduly concerned. Flattered by the valuation, which had been leaked, and which was only £4,000 less than their asking price, they felt that

> we need not worry very much whether the Corporation sees fit to reopen the question again or not, because we find that the Company, as far as we can see, is on a very comfortable and safe footing.

The Great War and the Tramways

The effect of wartime conditions on the tramway infrastructure was to postpone the routine replacement of trams and track beyond the fifteen-year life which had been assumed for them, and to create a backlog of repairs on both.

The First World War had a profound effect on the tramways, and on the men who worked for the Department. Shortages had led to a decline in standards of maintenance of the trams and the tracks upon which they ran, so that the tramways lost their high-quality image. This was particularly true of the Suburban Tramways Company, whose undertaking had become particularly decrepit. Price and wage inflation during the war made it clear that pressures, both upward and downward, would apply after the war.

Brush car 14 fitted with a folding windscreen, angled to avoid the brake handle, at Bridge of Dee terminus during the First World War. This car survived as a YMCA caravan at Park, on Deeside, until it was destroyed following a failed preservation attempt in the 1960s.

Brush 12 was a Torry car and is seen at St Fittick's Road terminus during the First World War.

1914 Brush car 81 during the First World War at Mannofield with a conductress. It kept its 'Pay As You Enter' reversed-stair layout until 1923 and was withdrawn in 1950.

Early Corporation Bus Services

It would have been surprising if Pilcher had not been aware of the possibilities of bus operation as a means of extending at low cost the municipal transport network, and in May 1913 a Provisional Order was promoted by the Town Council to authorise the operation of motor bus routes outside the city boundary. The routes were tours rather than local services and were in response to the growing demand for 'excursions' to local beauty spots, but the outbreak of the First World War prevented their introduction.

On the other hand, vehicle technology advanced quickly, and mass-production of vehicles led to more efficient, lower-cost methods of assembly. More significantly, demobilisation of large numbers of young men, many with mechanical and driving skills, together with the disposal of many almost-new army vehicles in an economy with rising unemployment, led to a rapid increase in the number of small-scale entrants to the market.

The Suburban after the First World War

By the beginning of 1923 it was obvious that if the Suburban was to stay in business as a tramway operator, it would have to invest in some new equipment. The newest of the trams was nine years old and the majority of them were ten years older than that. The state of the track was giving rise to protracted battles by letter with the Aberdeen District Committee. The total bill for the Suburban was estimated at £6,540. Desperately casting around for a solution, which would avoid having to spend any money, the Suburban Board remembered that Aberdeen Corporation had merely deferred the question of purchase in 1916, so they wrote to the Town Council to see if they were still interested. Losing no time, the Corporation commissioned another report from the tramways manager, by now William Forbes, and applied for a Draft Order to authorise purchase, notified in the *Edinburgh Gazette* on 23 March 1923.

Forbes was rather less enthusiastic about purchase than Pilcher had been, not surprisingly in view of the run-down state of the equipment. Despite this, he reported that

> it may reasonably be expected ... that if and when the Corporation take over the undertaking of the Suburban Company the improvement effected in the permanent way, the rolling stock, etc., will create a large amount of new traffic so that within a short time the estimated loss will be turned into a considerable profit.

Despite the defects in the report (the most obvious being the notion that a profit could be made on Suburban routes effectively restored to 1904 condition, single track and all) and the valuation of only £15,619 including the buses, the Corporation immediately made the very handsome offer of £30,000, subject to the passage of the Provisional Order through Parliament, and the County's agreement. The date of transfer was to be 23 July 1923.

Amazingly, the Suburban replied on 23 March that the offer was 'not one which the directors of the Company can submit for the approval of the shareholders'. This really was the last chance for the Suburban, and it is hard to resist the conclusion that the Suburban directors must either have known very little about the condition of their business, or have completely misjudged the mood of the Corporation. Thereafter the story became a struggle for survival in the face of increasing odds.

Driver Barbara Craib had initially sought work with Lanarkshire Tramways, but when the Suburban began hiring female staff during the First World War she returned home. (B. Anderson)

Suburban car 4 was one of four Brush covered-top trams purchased for the opening of the line in 1904. They had fifty-eight seats and an unusual saloon design when new which had a section for non-smokers with comfy padded seats, while smokers had to endure slatted wooden benches and no outer door. This explains the odd window arrangement. By the date of this photo, taken during the First World War, the smokers had been banished to the top deck. (First Aberdeen)

The last tram purchased by the Suburban, in May 1914, was 11, seen here at Bieldside terminus during the First World War. It was reputedly the most popular car among the crews and the most reliable. It was the last tram on the Deeside route, and survived as a summer house at Ellon until being rescued for use on the Alford Valley Railway, where it can be seen today. Note the detailed railway timetable at the tram stop, advertising the competing Suburban train service which the LNER abandoned in 1937.

At the end of the Suburban's existence the cars were in a very poor state. Even though 1904 car 2 is a battered relic, the driver is still smart in his white-topped cap in this view at Bucksburn. While the legal dispute with Aberdeen Corporation dragged out, one Suburban car a day travelled over each route to maintain the operation. This stopped soon after the case was lost by the Suburban on 4 June 1927. (Postcard)

Corporation Lines after the First World War

The demobilisation of the armed forces had led to a surplus in the labour market and, as well as leading to a reduction in wage levels, it also resulted in a sharp rise in the number of unemployed. The total reached 6,000 in Aberdeen in March 1921, and led to calls for unemployment relief schemes.

The line to Hazlehead might not have been built if the Scottish Office had not approved a 50 per cent grant of the cost as an unemployment relief measure, provided construction was in hand by the end of February 1924, and complete within nine months. Work started from both ends on 6 March, and opened on 16 July. The line was inspected by Col Pringle for the Ministry of Transport on 24 July 1924. Fittingly, the opening of the Hazlehead extension, thereby bringing the system (including the Suburban lines) to its maximum extent, was closely followed on 1 August 1924 by the parade to mark the Jubilee of the Tramways.

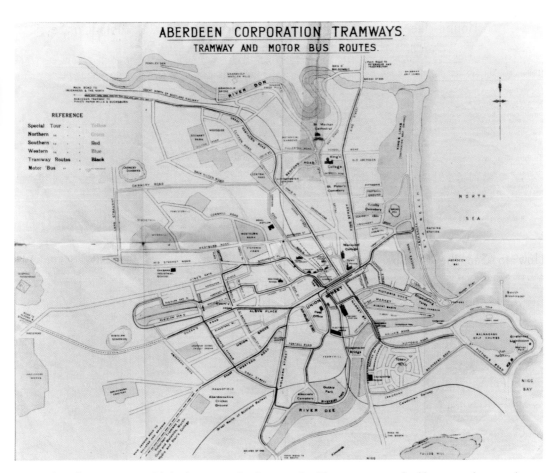

When this map was published in 1922, the Corporation Tramway routes had been supplemented by one regular bus route (from Garden City to Footdee – shown dotted black) and four tour bus routes. (First Aberdeen)

84 was built at Dee Village Road, Ferryhill, in 1918 for the Sea Beach route as an unemployment relief scheme. Although only a fifty-four-seater, it and its two sisters were nicknamed 'monsters'. Again, the official ACT view is on Whinhill Road. It only lasted in passenger service until 1932/33, when (still open-topped) it was converted to a salt-spreading car. It was scrapped in mid-1952. (First Aberdeen)

61 was a 1922 ACT-built car, fitted with a vestibule from new. Along with 57–60, it was built 'to prevent unemployment in the workshops' and used second-hand components from 1899 cars 1–3 and 'narrow cars' 21–24. Seen here at Fountainhall Road, it was described in the press as being painted in a 'nice fast colour', but that must have been the only fast thing about it, as it was referred to in a post-war rolling stock report as a 'slow tram only suitable for the Woodside Fountain service'.

The new route to Hazlehead was opened on 16 July 1924 by 1920 Corporation-built car 92. It survived the Second World War, being broken up at King Street depot in April 1955.

The General Strike

The General Strike has been described as 'one of the most controversial and significant events of the inter-war years' and, presumably because of the enormous response, as 'a great success' by some historians, but as 'the tragedy that took place in the month of May about which the less said the better' by Hugh Lyon, general secretary of the Scottish Horse and Motormen's Association at the time. The strike was certainly a personal disaster for many of the Aberdeen tramwaymen because of the loss of their pensions, and effectively neutralised union activity in the Department for years. Nevertheless the events of May 1926 still form a crucial element in the folklore of the Labour movement. Locally, it was to be the only occasion when the Corporation tramways employees came out on strike.

While limited services were provided by the Corporation, largely using inspectors, non-union cleaners and student volunteers provided by a sympathetic university administration, it was noticeable that the services attempted were largely in the affluent west end of the city, where transport was still required. No service ran to Torry or Footdee (serving the shipyards) until Monday 10 May. Volunteer platform staff were confined to the buses, where virtually instant driving and tram-conducting training was given. An attempt to introduce student tram drivers was greeted by a threat from the inspectors that they would join the strike, though this was met by a counter-threat of mass dismissal. Perhaps fortunately for both sides, a planned training session for students on Great Western Road on Sunday 9 May had to be cancelled because no power was available, and students were never used to drive the trams.

An interesting feature of the strike in Aberdeen was the attempt made by both sides to contain any violence, the Corporation by arranging police protection for the crews, the Strike Committee by seeking to agree an authorised service. The attempt was largely unsuccessful. The first instance of violence occurred on Thursday 6 May, when the drivers of three buses on the Union Grove service were 'forcibly removed from their posts and the buses driven back to the depot by the strikers'. It is interesting that the strikers felt it necessary to drive the buses back to the depot. Potentially far more serious were two sabotage attempts – on the same day, a fourth bus broke down immediately after leaving the Constitution Street depot because a cigarette end dropped into the petrol tank had been sucked into the carburettor, and one of the three buses on service had its magneto put out of adjustment. When the garage superintendent arrived in Union Grove to install a replacement magneto, 'a hostile crowd was present but allowed him to effect repairs and escorted the bus back to the garage'. A planned skeleton service of tramcars on the Woodside route (joint with the Aberdeen Suburban Company), Mannofield, Rosemount and part of the Bridges routes, using ten vehicles, was abandoned because 'a hostile crowd numbering over 1,000 was at Queens Cross when the cars were due to leave and it would have been a very difficult matter to have got the cars out in view of the threatening attitude of those present'.

The General Strike was called off by the TUC late on Wednesday 12 May, but the Corporation's threat to reinstate only a limited number of strikers after the deadline was carried out. The combined effect of intensive pirate bus competition, a stringent economy drive and fuel shortages led to a reduction in the normal requirement of trams by twelve to eighty-six, which in turn meant that ninety-seven out of the total workforce of 639 would not be required.

Students In "Charge."

The Aberdeen students rallied to the call for volunteers and manned the buses with great spirit. Here are two of them who filled the roles of driver and conductor of a Corporation bus.

Students with a police escort during the General Strike in 1926 in this fuzzy *Bon-Accord* magazine report. 5 (RS7005) was a 1925 Shinnie-bodied Thorneycroft.

Pirate Buses and Fleet Renewals

The debate on the future of the tram or the bus continued until well after the Second World War; the debate was, however, greatly intensified by the onset of serious competition from independent operators from 1925.

The 'pirate bus wars' of the 1920s have usually been characterised as episodes of intense and unrestricted competition, with 'unfair' practices being used by the independent bus proprietors against the 'responsible' incumbent municipalities. Allegations were made at the time that the 'pirates' only operated when the traffic on offer was greatest, that buses were turned short, with passengers turned out, that reliability was poor, wages low, and safety standards dangerously inadequate. The real situation was undoubtedly more complex. There were instances of the abuses listed, and some companies were less responsible than others. Corners were inevitably cut in the search for viability. But it was by no means only the pirates who were liable to resort to corner-cutting in the intense competition of the mid-1920s. For example, Aberdeen Tramways Department routinely turned 'duplicate' vehicles out in front of Rover Bus Service vehicles at several points on the route from Rosemount to Bay of Nigg, and turned short if few passengers were gained, while it was normal practice to race back to the Wallace Statue with the conductor perched on the front lamp bracket resetting the destination indicator.

Omnibus Bye-Laws had been made by Aberdeen Corporation in September 1926, soon after the first major surge of competition appeared, but these were not approved and confirmed by the Sheriff until October 1927. The most potent provision, and that which effectively removed the remaining pirate opposition from the tramways, was a provision which prohibited buses from stopping at tramway stops, though strict police enforcement of the vehicle safety provisions, and the use by the magistrates of their power to refuse a licence on road congestion grounds undoubtedly helped. Between 3 November 1927 and the end of the year, four of the pirate operators had ceased because of their inability to use tram stops. This device, which was unique in Scotland to Aberdeen, demonstrated the determination of the city to take measures to protect its municipal transport operation from competition.

The pirate bus war in Aberdeen effectively lasted from May 1925 to November 1927, and involved at most thirty competing buses. While this number of vehicles appears small, it must be remembered that the Corporation bus and tram fleets at this period numbered only 36 and 110 respectively.

The financial effect on the Corporation tramways was the most obvious and immediate. Less obvious was the effect on the relative importance of the Corporation tram and bus fleets. It was 1927 which saw the greatest fall in tramway receipts, by 19 per cent. Revenue on tram routes recovered during 1928 and 1929 to a level only 9 per cent below that of 1925, while Corporation bus receipts increased by 48 per cent. Since much of the increase in bus traffic was contributed by the increasing population of the new housing estates, population which had formerly been located on the tram routes, part of the reduction in the tram receipts was due to a structural change in the customer base, and represented a permanent shift in demand from tram routes to bus routes.

By the 1930s the bus route network was as extensive as the tramways. Notable is the extent to which the city had spread to the north and west, and how many of the bus routes duplicated tramway services. (First Aberdeen)

111, a 1925 Brush-built tram on route 2 to Mannofield, stars in a Union Street dominated by public transport. Nearly a dozen trams, three buses and three taxis outnumber the solitary private car (in front of the second bus). Bus 6 (RS3716) is a 1921 Thorneycroft J with Aberdeen Corporation body. (Postcard)

The Rosemount Circle was numbered 5 in the anti-clockwise direction (via Kings Gate) and 3 in the clockwise direction (via Queens Cross), though this clockwise tram was probably returning from a Kings Gate short working. 117 was one of a series of nine trams built by Aberdeen Corporation between 1926 and 1931. This one was built at Dee Village Road workshops in Ferryhill in 1926. By now, its original Brill 21E truck had been replaced by a Peckham P35. (RJS Wiseman)

Another of the 1926–31 batch of Aberdeen Corporation-built cars was 118, seen here on a Sea Beach extra working on route 9 to Holburn Junction. It is followed by 92 (which opened the Hazlehead route) on a Bridges peak extra working, a 'London RT'-style AEC Regent III of 1946 and a Bogie streamliner. (RJS Wiseman)

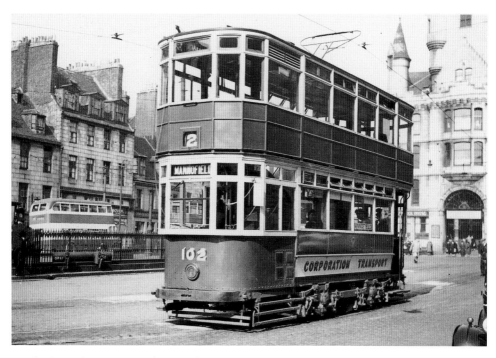

102 basks in the sun at Castle Street loop, awaiting departure for Mannofield. 102 was one of six cars built by Aberdeen Corporation in 1925, but this is actually the 1927-built car 120, with which 102 exchanged numbers in the early 1930s for some reason!

132 was one of the twelve Brush all-enclosed cars bought in 1929. Nicknamed 'English Cars', this one ran the Sea Beach emergency service when the route was reopened during the Suez fuel crisis. It is seen here on Constitution Street. (RJS Wiseman)

'English Car' 132 in Rosemount on a short working to Kings Gate in January 1952. (RJS Wiseman)

A spectacular example of what head-to-head competition between rival bus firms could result in was captured by *Bon Accord* magazine. This was the result of an accident involving 'Radio' and 'Bydand' buses in Union Street on 11 June 1929. (*Bon Accord & Northern Pictorial*)

More Corporation Buses and the First Tram Closures

With the opening of the Hazlehead extension to the Bayview route in 1924, the tramway system was at its greatest extent. In 1927, after a period of severe bus competition from both its own buses and those of Bydand Motor Transport, and disruption of its Deeside route tracks by roadworks in connection with the Invercannie aqueduct, the Aberdeen Suburban Tramways services to Bieldside and Bankhead were abandoned in July 1927, leaving Corporation cars only on the routes to Woodside and Mannofield. The operating results of the Torry and Ferryhill lines were affected by bus competition (both from independents and from the Corporation's own vehicles), and the climate of opinion was very much against tramway expansion, if it had not yet turned conclusively towards wholesale abandonment.

The bus route network, on the other hand, was expanding rapidly to serve the developing Corporation housing estates at Torry and Hilton, as the population was being dispersed away from the area around the tramway routes. In terms of mileage operated, the buses surpassed the trams in 1932, though in terms of passengers carried the trams still carried 5.5 million more, at 41.4 million in 1939.

The number of buses in the fleet stood at 73 in May 1930; by May 1939 this had increased to 111 larger buses, with almost half being double-decked.

After the withdrawal of the Ferryhill and Torry routes in the early 1930s, it was still the tram fleet, and the tram route network, which were seen as the backbone of the system, handling the main traffic flows on very high frequencies, dealing with Bank Holiday crowds, and the summer rush to the Beach and Hazlehead. The buses were seen, in contrast, as the means by which the developing new housing estates could be served, as well as providing relatively wide-interval services to low-density areas such as Nigg, Midstocket, Forresterhill and Thorngrove. The tram fleet, after the major overhaul programme of the late 1920s, and the purchase of the twelve new English Electric cars in 1929, was in good condition. Indeed, the fleet was rather too large for the services then operated, since only a limited number of cars had been withdrawn after the Ferryhill and Torry closures. Yet the development of the tram system did not cease, though extensions were confined to improving the terminal arrangements at Castle Street in 1935 and 1937, creating a loop line at Pittodrie for football trams in 1937, and undertaking a short extension of the Woodside route to Scatterburn in July 1938, to cater for the new Middlefield housing scheme. An ambitious scheme to lay a new road and tramway to the Beach was interrupted by the war, and was destined never to be resumed.

The End of the Torry and Ferryhill Trams

The issue which brought the debate to a head in Aberdeen was the proposed abandonment of the Torry and Ferryhill tram routes. The Ferryhill route in particular had never been a strong route financially, and both it and the Torry route had suffered dramatic decreases in passengers due to the introduction of new bus routes. In the case of the Torry route, these difficulties were exacerbated by the long-standing source of delay to trams on the single-track section across the quays, and the urgent need for renewal of the track, which dated from the original installation in 1903.

The Torry route trams ran for the last time on 28 February 1931.

Abandonment of the Ferryhill route was altogether more contentious. The Tramways Committee's decision for abandonment was referred back by the full Council before being passed again by the Committee and finally ratified.

TORRY ROUTE

No. 8. *Commenced 10th October 1903*
~~Finished~~ 28th April 1931

Passengers are requested to note that the **TORRY CAR SERVICE** will be withdrawn on the night of SATURDAY, 28th instant, and commencing on SUNDAY, 1st MARCH, 1931, a service of Motor Buses will be operated from **Wallace Statue** to **St. Fitticks Road**, via **Union Terrace, Union Street, Market Street,** and **Victoria Road.**

SERVICE :

MONDAY to FRIDAY,	...	...	...	5 mins. all day.
SATURDAY,	...	...	...	{5 „ till 12 noon. {4 „ till 11·10 p.m.
SUNDAY,	...	...	...	6 „ all day.

	Monday to Friday		Saturday		Sunday	
	First Bus	Last Bus	First Bus	Last Bus	First Bus	Last Bus
Wallace Statue to St. Fitticks Road,	7·10 a.m.	11·0 p.m.	7·10 a.m.	11·10 p.m.	9·54 a.m.	10·12 p.m.
St. Fitticks Road to Wallace Statue,	7·23 a.m.	11·13 p.m.	7·23 a.m.	11·22 p.m.	10·6 a.m.	10·24 p.m.

FARES : Wallace Statue to Mansefield Road
Trinity Quay to Baxter Street -   - } **1d.**
Commercial Quay to St. Fitticks Rd.

 Statue to St. Fitticks Road, **1½d.**

Torry route closure notice. (First Aberdeen)

Tram Fleet Renewal 1930-39

Although the tram fleet was in generally good condition by the 1930s, there were still a large number of trams in service which dated from before the First World War, and many of the later trams were technically obsolete. As a result of the closure of the Ferryhill and Torry routes, the pressure for fleet replacement had been lessened, but if the tramway system were to continue on its current scale it would be necessary to replace these cars at an early date. Perhaps fortuitously, but possibly at the suggestion of the former Aberdeen general manager, J. L. Gunn, now manager at Nottingham, a number of relatively recent tramcars became available from Nottingham Corporation, and nineteen of these were purchased at £195 each, delivered.

While it would have been possible to continue to purchase second-hand trams from tram systems which were being closed down, it was clear that such a policy could not form the basis for a long-term fleet renewal programme, and with the active and personal support of Transport Convener Collins, the general manager submitted a report which recommended the purchase of twenty new trams and thirty sets of air brakes to bring the tram fleet up to date. Tenders were received from the English Electric Company for two bogie trams and two four-wheel trams, at a total of £13,878. It is worth noting that a fifty-six-seat double-deck bus of the period would have cost £1,970 complete, and that the cost of providing the same seating capacity would have been £9,850, though the vehicle life would have been ten years compared with thirty. On a straight-line depreciation, the comparative costs per annum were trams: £463, buses: £985. Thus the choice made was an apparently good one, but with its correctness dependant on the continuation of the tramway system.

The first batch of second-hand trams to arrive in Aberdeen were nineteen four-wheelers dating from 1926 which had been displaced at Nottingham. One was used for spares and the rest entered service as 1–18. Here, the first one to be refurbished is inspected by the Tramways Committee in December 1936. They were all withdrawn between 1949 and 1951.

The Nottingham cars were regular performers on the Mannofield route. Car 2 is seen here shortly before the Second World War, crossing Union Bridge.

In 1940, English Electric built four streamlined prototype trams for Aberdeen, based on the Blackpool 'balloon' car design of 1933. Two (138 and 139) were bogie cars, while the other two (140 and 141) were sixty-four-seat four-wheelers. 141 is awaiting delivery at Preston works in July 1940. It worked on the Woodside and Mannofield routes and then was stored out of service until it was burnt along with the rest of the fleet in May 1958. (English Electric)

Changes in Attitude to the Trams

The final report of the Royal Commission on Transport in 1929 devoted a chapter to 'Tramways and Trackless Trolley Vehicles', and drew a number of conclusions on the future of tramways. While admitting that 'under favourable conditions, they are an essential method of road passenger transport', the tramcar 'possesses certain disadvantages so serious that we think it probable that had the motor omnibus been invented at the time when tramways were first authorised not a single mile of tramway would ever have been laid down'.

The Road Traffic Act did not, however, take on board the criticism of tramways levelled by the Royal Commission of 1929. Of more influence on transport developments in towns were opinion-formers in the industry itself. Prominent among these was the former Aberdeen general manager, Pilcher, who had moved on to the prestigious position of general manager of Edinburgh Corporation Tramways, and was widely regarded as being in the forefront of transport management techniques. As early as 1920, Pilcher had begun to question the feasibility of renewing the track on routes which could be more efficiently worked with buses.

The last Ferryhill tram ran on 31 May 1931, once eight second-hand single-deck buses were obtained from Glasgow Corporation. Although a report to the Tramways Permanent Way Sub-Committee in August 1928 had made it clear that, apart from the Mannofield route and Union Street, practically the whole tramways needed to be relaid, the abandonments of the Torry and Ferryhill routes seem to have been regarded generally as isolated issues rather than implying the adoption of a wholesale abandonment of the system. A batch of twelve new tramcars had been purchased in 1929, and sixteen others had undergone major reconstruction, demonstrating continued commitment to the tramways.

The Second World War and the Effect on Post-War Transport Policy

> We are convinced that the tram is still the most popular and best mode of transport.
> The new vehicles are the last word in trams. They will provide luxury travel. They are
> the best yet made, ahead of Glasgow's streamlined Coronation cars.

So said Transport Convener Collins at the Transport Committee meeting which recommended purchase of the new English Electric trams in June 1939. Glasgow, he said, had decided to spend £1 million on new trams after finding trolleybuses unsuitable.

When the new trams arrived in July 1940, *Bon Accord*'s headline was 'Glasgow has nothing to crow about now'. The commentary added, 'Aberdeen hearts will swell with civic pride when this streamlined beauty goes into service soon.' Yet only a few years later, the clamour to replace the trams had grown to the point where, despite the delivery of a further twenty of the same vehicles, the Council agreed to their complete abandonment.

The effects of the Second World War on the Transport Department were even more dramatic than had been experienced during the Great War; in 1940 a 50 per cent cut in bus route mileage, involving a 40 per cent cut in the bus fleet, had been enforced, and though many of the buses requisitioned by the War Department and allocated to the Air Raid Precautions organisation for service as ambulances, mortuaries or troop transports were the oldest vehicles, some of the newest single-decks were taken. In addition, in 1940, a small number of double-deckers were sent to London for a time, while loans were also made to Glasgow to replace war-damaged vehicles. The route structure was changed at the same time so that, as far as possible, bus routes acted as feeders to the tram routes. Shortages of materials and of skilled labour exacerbated the problem of maintaining an ageing fleet which was being worked harder, and breakdowns became common.

During the war, the manufacture of guns, tanks, warships and planes had top priority, yet civilian life had to go on, and in particular war workers needed public transport. Supplies of new buses virtually ceased, and operators were soon finding difficulties in meeting the requirement for serviceable vehicles. Aberdeen suffered relatively little bomb damage, with only one tram suffering serious damage while on service in King Street, and the needs of the Transport Department for new vehicles were therefore comparatively light.

Lack of maintenance and labour shortages during the Second World War led to a decline in the condition and appearance of the fleet. In this interesting view, the 'Emergency car' of 1904 is assisting ex-Nottingham 3, which has suffered a broken axle at Holburn Junction, while 127 waits on Alford Place. The emergency car was painted all-over blue and lasted until 1952.

A vintage tram line-up at King Street depot just after the Second World War. 27 was a 1902 BEC car, 4a was an 1899 ex-Woodside car by now relegated to spreading salt, while ex-Nottingham 3 and 1 were in the twilight of their years. (Hector Mackenzie)

Planning for a Post-War Aberdeen

The major influence on transport requirement, after the Second World War was the development of new council housing estates beyond the traditional settlement areas.

After the Second World War the pressure for accelerated housing construction was even greater, since in the period 1940–5 no private housing had been built, and only 852 Corporation houses, of which over 200 were completions of projects already under way at the outbreak of war. In addition, some 200 houses had been destroyed in air raids, or had been so badly damaged as to require subsequent demolition.

Post-War Transport Policy: Trams in the Balance

The general manager, Alfred Smith, reported to the Transport Committee in July 1946 on the reinstatement and development of pre-war bus routes, and on the proposed purchase of twenty new trams as well as fifteen second-hand trams from Manchester. However, at nearly £8,500 each, and in the current state of debate on the issue, the twenty new trams failed to get approval from the full Council at the first attempt, and had to await the full report on the future of the undertaking which the general manager submitted in December 1945. Because English Electric (who had built the prototypes in 1939–40) were no longer able to fulfil the order, an approach was made to Glasgow Corporation to build twenty of their 'Coronation' trams. Only because this would have been outside the legal powers of the Glasgow undertaking was the order finally given to R. Y. Pickering of Wishaw. Had Glasgow Corporation been given the order, it is fair to assume that Aberdeen would have participated in some of the economies of scale (for example in the purchase of trucks) which Glasgow achieved.

Trolleybuses were dismissed in the report as costly to install and operate, while the option of substituting buses for trams was estimated to increase operating costs, principally due to the shorter vehicle life of buses and because the option would also involve the writing off of large amounts of capital investment in the tramways.

A further factor leading to a questioning of future transport policy in the late 1940s and early 1950s was the financial performance of the undertaking. For the first time in its existence, the tramways made an operating loss of over £19,000 in 1947 while the buses, after having returned an operating loss of £4,000 in 1945, made small profits in both 1946 and 1947. In each of the following six years, the buses made considerable operating losses, while the trams lost comparable sums in the first five of these years.

The reason for the sudden downturn was not hard to find. The Department faced a dilemma; the total market had greatly increased, but this growth had produced an increase in revenue per mile which was greatly exceeded by the growth in operating cost per mile. While most of the extra mileage run was on the trams, pressures were building up for rapid expansion of the bus network to serve the new estates, which would have the effect of increasing bus mileage faster than the growth in passengers. The immediate answer to the problem of inadequate revenue was to raise the fares. Unfortunately, this was not a simple process, since the Traffic Commissioner exercised control over prices under the 1930 Act.

The second batch of second-hand trams were fourteen 'Pilcher' cars purchased from Manchester Corporation in 1949. Manchester 270 became 48 at Aberdeen and was in service from April 1949 to October 1955.

Pilcher 48 on temporary track at Rubislaw on route 4. Notorious for 'tail-wagging' at speed, they were used as peak extras.

Although English Electric had built the four 1940 experimental cars, they were no longer producing trams by 1949 and eventually (after exploring the possible purchase of Glasgow 'Coronations') Aberdeen ordered twenty new cars to English Electric pattern from Pickering of Wishaw. Less than ten years later this car was sold for scrap for £90. Here, one of the new Aberdeen bogie cars leaves Wishaw for Aberdeen.

Bogie 19 in King Street depot yard in January 1949. It was in service on the last day of trams in Aberdeen, 3 May 1958. An attempt was made to purchase sister car 36 for preservation, but was defeated by the refusal of the Transport Department to store the vehicle at King Street. (First Aberdeen)

The top deck (also of 19) was extremely light and airy, and gave an unrivalled view of the 'granite city' on a sunny day. Leather seats were provided upstairs and moquette downstairs in these days of smoking on the top deck. (First Aberdeen)

The lower deck of bogie car 19 when new. The intimidating notice to passengers is dated 1936. (First Aberdeen)

Bogie 27 at Music Hall shortly after delivery. Oddly, although the cars were fitted with separate route number indicators, the destination indicator also included the number. After a time, the route number indicators were painted over. (Postcard)

Bridge of Dee was the transfer point from the Bridges tram route to buses serving the new Garthdee and Kaimhill housing estates. 161 is a 1951 Daimler CVG6 with Northern Coachbuilders body. The bogie trams had a reputation for unreliability, and here a broken-down car receives help from the recovery truck, codenamed 'Oscar' on the ACT radio network, while another bogie car transfers passengers. (Hector Mackenzie)

The Royal Highland Show was a major crowd attractor at Hazlehead when it was held in Aberdeen before moving to its permanent home at Ingliston, near Edinburgh Airport. 122 was a home-built Standard of 1929 which was withdrawn in November 1955 after the Woodside route closed. (C. Carter)

Castle Street in the early 1950s, with bus 103, Pilcher 39, bus 67, 129 and bogie car. (First Aberdeen)

The End of the Trams

A major blow for the tramways was the death of Collins on 12 November 1950, though it was clear by this time that opinion was steadily hardening against continued tramway operation. Complaints were mounting that the new estates at Garthdee and Balgownie were not properly served by the single-deck shuttle-buses which connected with the Bridges route trams at Bridge of Dee and Bridge of Don, and opposition councillors took the opportunity to propose once again that the trams be scrapped. By January 1951, the Council had decided in principle that the Beach tramway should be abandoned within five years, and that the part-completed direct line to Sea Beach built just before the war, along what is now the Beach Boulevard, should be removed.

The deficit problem had already been addressed by a combination of service reductions and fare increases. However, as more bus services passed through Rosemount, the loadings of the Rosemount Circle tram route began to be affected. This, taken together with the unsuitability of the route for the new bogie trams because of the tight curves at South Mount Street and elsewhere, made the route an obvious candidate for conversion to buses, and this was carried in Council in July 1954, with closure taking place on 2 October.

With the closure of the Rosemount route, the tramway routes which now remained were:

1 Bridge of Dee–Bridge of Don
7 Scatterburn–Market Street
9 Hazlehead–Castle Street/Sea Beach

Of these, the Scatterburn route, although heavily used, suffered from the St Nicholas Street bottleneck, and could not accommodate the bogie trams, while the Sea Beach route had already been scheduled for closure. New housing estates were being built beyond the termini of the Bridges route, and the Hazlehead route was never a strong performer, except in summer. The bogie trams had proved an expensive disappointment; initially, before power-operated doors were fitted, two conductors had to be employed, making them expensive to operate, while their increased weight and mechanical complexity had contributed nothing to checking the increase in tram maintenance costs. Although popular with the passengers because they were warm and comfortable, with none of the draughts of the older cars' open platforms, the centre entrances with access to two saloons on the lower deck, and two staircases to the top deck caused congestion in loading and unloading. The cars had belatedly been found to be incapable of negotiating curves on the Rosemount and Woodside routes, so that their use had effectively to be limited to the Bridges, Sea Beach and Hazlehead routes, and the low-slung running gear tended to 'ground' on any serious track imperfections, or on packed ice in winter. In short, the new trams were unsuitable for the Aberdeen system. As the unsuitability of the new trams became obvious to the Transport Department, and no doubt to the more interested politicians on the Transport Committee, the debacle had the effect of discrediting any investment in the tramways. It came as no surprise, therefore, that in June 1954 the Town Council remitted the general manager, F. Y. Frazer, to 'prepare ... a report containing proposals for the abandonment ... of the remaining tramcar services operated by the Transport Undertaking and for the replacement thereof by omnibus services'.

The Frazer Report of 12 January 1955 acknowledged the use of home-produced electricity by the trams, and the benefits of low step heights for the elderly, as well as smoothness of running and lack of exhaust gases, were acknowledged, but Frazer also claimed that the diesel for the replacement buses would be 'produced in Scotland' (by which he presumably meant that it would be refined at Grangemouth), while of the eight remaining tram-operating municipalities, four had already decided to abandon their tramways, and all the others were implementing fleet reductions. He concluded by recommending a phased abandonment to allow the absorption of existing tramway staff into the bus establishment, and to avoid an unduly large intake of buses in one year, with later fleet-age profile problems.

The reaction of the people of Aberdeen to the tram scrapping issue, which was clearly gathering momentum, seems to have been a mixture of nostalgia and approval. The closure of the Mannofield route in 1951 appears to have occurred without any ceremony, though the closure of the Rosemount Circle in 1954, with a closure procession led by the remaining horse tram, attracted large crowds. After criticism in the press of the extravagance involved in getting that horse tram restored, however, the Woodside and Beach/Hazlehead routes were closed without official ceremony. Only when the final conversion of the Bridges route was due, in May 1958, was another major procession held. Within a few days of the closure, all the remaining tramcars, which had been sold to Birds Commercial Motors of Stratford, were burnt on the Sea Beach reserved track section. Only one tram – the converted ex-horse tram *No.1*, which had been used in the final closure procession – was retained, thanks to the intervention of Edinburgh Corporation, which offered to keep it (and transport it at their expense to Edinburgh).

A 1955 Crossley-bodied Daimler CVG6 on route 22 (Northfield) passes a tram instruction board on the Rosemount Circle, which closed in October 1954. The shield shape was a characteristic of Aberdeen tram (and bus) signs until the 1960s. Trams stopped at 'stations', while buses called at 'stops', while in the city centre, passengers were instructed to 'Q 2 deep'. (Hector Mackenzie)

Cleaning grooves at Kittybrewster was one of the most unglamourous aspects of track maintenance. (Hector Mackenzie)

The winter of 1957/58 was a severe one, and several withdrawn standards were pressed into service as snowploughs. Here, 62 clears the way for a bogie car in Holburn Street. (Hector Mackenzie)

After one of the two nights of the fire at the Beach reserved track, the remains of two standards cool down in the morning sun.

Bibliography

This book is by its nature a brief summary of the history of the tramways of Aberdeenshire. For more detail the reader is referred to the principal published works on the tramways covered in this book, which are as follows:

Aberdeen (District, Corporation and Suburban)

Mitchell, M. J. and I. A. Souter, *Aberdeen District Tramways* (Dundee: NB Traction, 1983).

Mitchell, M. J., *Fae Dee to Don & Back Again: 100 Years of Public Transport in Aberdeen* (Aberdeen: First Aberdeen Ltd, 1998).

Mitchell, M. J. and I. A. Souter, *Aberdeen Suburban Tramways* (Dundee: NB Traction, 1980).

These three books are detailed accounts of the tramways and buses operated by Aberdeen District Tramways, Aberdeen Corporation Transport and Aberdeen Suburban Tramways. An excellent photographic survey is:

Brotchie, A., *Twilight Years of the Trams in Aberdeen and Dundee* (Brora: Adam Gordon, 2003).

Skene & Echt Schemes

Mitchell, M. J., 'The Skene & Echt Railway Schemes', *Great North Review*, 4 (14) (Aug. 1967) and 5 (16) (Feb. 1968).

Nicoll, E., 'Proposed Echt Light Railway', *Great North Review*, 27 (2) 106 and 107 (Summer/Autumn 1990).

Cruden Bay Hotel Tramway

Mitchell, M. J., 'The Cruden Bay Hotel and its Tramway', *Great North Review*, (Nov. 1979), pp. 57–64.
Jones, K. G., *The Cruden Bay Hotel and its Tramway* (Alford: Grampian Transport Museum, 2004).

Strabathie Light Railway

Pirie, A. G., 'The Strabathie Light Railway', *Railway Archive*, 17 (Witney: Lightmoor Press, 2007), pp. 5–23.